HAMSTERS

Sandie Lee Books

Hamsters

The first hamsters were found deep under the ground in the Middle East. That was in 1930. These hamsters were taken into a lab and allowed to reproduce. In 1938, the hamsters were taken to the United States to be used for medical testing. However, by 1947, these cute critters were being kept as pets. There are 25 different species of the hamster. Let's explore more cool and fascinating facts about these neat little animals. Read on…

Where in the World?

Did you know wild hamsters live in Syria? These dirt-dwellers live under the ground where they are safe from predators. They are considered rodents and belong to the subfamily of Cricetinae. They like to live in desert regions or semi-arid areas. These places also include Europe, Asia and the Middle East.

The Body of a Hamster

Did you know unlike mice, hamsters have short stubby tails? These rodents have stout, furry bodies, small soft ears and black beady eyes. Their thick fur can be black, grey, white, brown, red, golden or a mix of all of these. The hamster has small feet with tiny toes and claws on each one.

The Hamster's Cheeks

Did you know hamsters have pouches? These are found on both sides of its face. They have 2 cheek pouches they use to take food and bedding materials back to their dens. It is like having built-in shopping bags! This helps keep the hamsters safe by not having to travel so much.

What a Hamster Eats

Did you know the hamster eats a variety of food? In the wild a hamster eats berries, nuts, seeds and veggies. Some will even dine on worms and various insects. If you keep a hamster as a pet, you can buy a pre-packaged seed mix. Hamsters also like to have peanuts and raisins as a special treat.

The Hamster's Home

Did you know a hamster can dig long tunnels? When a hamster lives in the wild, it will dig a burrow (nest) underground. This nest is at the end of at least 2 long tunnels. It will have separate places for its nest, food storage and other activities. For safety, the hamster will have at least two entrances.

The Hamster's Special Ability

Did you know the hamster can stay awake all night long? Hamsters are nocturnal. This means they prefer to sleep all day and stay awake at night. If you keep a hamster as a pet, you will probably hear it running on its wheel. This is great exercise for this energetic little critter.

The Hamster as Prey

Did you know hamsters are hunted by many predators? Because the hamster is so small, it makes it an easy catch for a lot of different predators. Snakes hunt the hamster along the ground and in its burrow. Birds of prey, cats and wild dogs will also hunt the hamster. Even some South American tribes dine on this rodent.

Hamster Trails

Did you know hamsters have very poor eyesight? Hamsters can see better up close than they can far away. This is called, nearsighted. Hamsters are also color blind. In the wild, hamsters leave scent trails so they can find their way back home. They do this by rubbing against things along the way.

Mom Hamster

Did you know a mother hamster can have dozens of babies over her lifetime? A female hamster is ready to have babies at 2 months of age. She is pregnant for 15 to 21 days. She can give birth from 4 to 7 babies. The most babies a mother hamster had at one time is 26!

Baby Hamsters

Did you know baby hamsters are called pups? Baby hamsters are very tiny when they are born. They are blind, without fur and totally helpless. By two weeks old, the pups have grown hair and their eyes are open. They will stop nursing milk from their mother at about 3 to 4 weeks-old.

Hamster Play

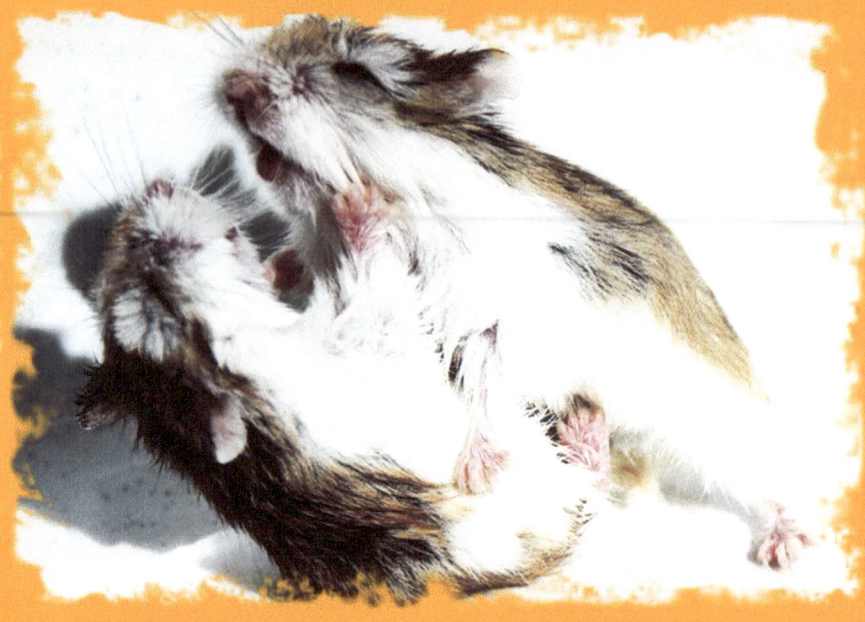

Did you know hamsters like to play? Hamsters live alone when they are adults, but they are still very active. Pet hamsters will run for hours on a wheel. They also like to chew up cardboard. Providing your hamster plastic tubes or recycled paper towel rolls will make them very happy.

Life of a Hamster

Did you know hamsters have a short lifespan? Due to so many predators, hamsters in the wild live only a short while. Pet hamsters can live from 2 to 3 years. It may not be a long time, but they make wonderful little pets. They are easy to care for and fun to play with.

The Dwarf Hamster

This species of the hamster is the smallest of them all - it only grows to be about 3 inches long! Depending on the type, this hamster can be white, grey or tan and may have stripes down its back. It is very active and can run for hours on a wheel.

Long-haired Hamster

This type of hamster has a long fur coat. It is soft and silky and comes in many different colors. The hair on the males tend to get longer than that on the female. These hamsters will need to have the bedding picked out of their fur, especially if you are using shavings, like cedar or pine.

Quiz

Question 1: In what year did the hamster begin being kept as a pet?

Answer 1: It was around 1947

Question 2: What feature does a hamster have, that a mouse does not?

Answer 2: A hamster's tail is short and stubby, rather than being long like a mouse

Question 3: How many entrances does a wild hamster have to its underground home?

Answer 3: It has two entrances

Question 4: Hamsters stay up all night long. What is this called?

Answer 4: Hamster's are nocturnal

Question 5: What are newborn hamsters called?

Answer 5: Pups

Thank you for checking out another addition from Sandie Lee Books! Make sure to check out Amazon.com for many other great titles.

www.ingramcontent.com/pod-product-compliance
Lightning Source LLC
Chambersburg PA
CBHW050801290526
45792CB00008B/2281